# THE
# RESURRECTION
### First Encounters with the Risen Christ

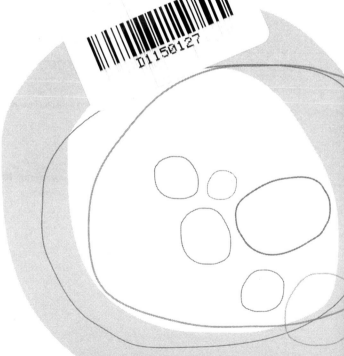

## Mark Meynell

The Resurrection
Mark Meynell and 10Publishing © 2013.

Published by 10Publishing, a division of 10ofThose Limited.
ISBN 9781906173715
Design and Typeset by: Mike Thorpe / www.design-chapel.com

Printed in the UK by CPI Group (UK) Ltd, Croydon, CR0 4YY

10Publishing, a division of 10ofthose.com
9D Centurion Court, Farrington, Leyland, PR25 3UQ, England.
Email: info@10ofthose.com
Website: www.10ofthose.com

# Dedication

For Joshua and Zanna
in True and Living Hope

# Contents

**1** Fears, Rumours and Doubts      1
Gloriously Overcome

**2** The Scriptures Must Be      18
Wonderfully Fulfilled

**3** Revolutionary Encounters      35
with the Risen Christ

# 1

# Fears, Rumours and Doubts Gloriously Overcome

## Matthew's Account of the Resurrection (Matt. 28)

After the Sabbath, at dawn on the first day of the week, Mary Magdalene and the other Mary went to look at the tomb.

2 There was a violent earthquake, for an angel of the Lord came down from heaven and, going to the tomb, rolled back the stone and sat on it. 3 His appearance was like lightning, and his clothes were white as snow. 4 The guards were so afraid of him that they shook and became like dead men.

5 The angel said to the women, 'Do not be afraid, for I know that you are looking for Jesus, who was crucified. 6 He is not here; he has risen, just as he said. Come and see the place where he lay. 7 Then go quickly and tell his disciples: "He has risen from the dead and is going ahead of you into Galilee. There you will see him." Now I have told you.'

8 So the women hurried away from the tomb, afraid yet filled with joy, and ran to tell his disciples. 9 Suddenly Jesus met them. 'Greetings,' he said. They

came to him, clasped his feet and worshipped him. [10] Then Jesus said to them, 'Do not be afraid. Go and tell my brothers to go to Galilee; there they will see me.'

[11] While the women were on their way, some of the guards went into the city and reported to the chief priests everything that had happened. [12] When the chief priests had met with the elders and devised a plan, they gave the soldiers a large sum of money, [13] telling them, 'You are to say, "His disciples came during the night and stole him away while we were asleep." [14] If this report gets to the governor, we will satisfy him and keep you out of trouble.' 15 So the soldiers took the money and did as they were instructed. And this story has been widely circulated among the Jews to this very day.

[16] Then the eleven disciples went to Galilee, to the mountain where Jesus had told them to go. [17] When they saw him, they worshipped him; but some doubted. [18] Then Jesus came to them and said, 'All authority in heaven and on earth has been given to me. [19] Therefore go and make disciples of all nations, baptising them in the name of the Father and of the Son and of the Holy Spirit, [20] and teaching them to obey everything I have commanded you. And surely I am with you always, to the very end of the age.'

When it's time for a General Election, a big question takes centre stage. How do you know who is telling the truth? How do you spot credibility, and more importantly, the lack of it?

Before you can make judgement calls, you need facts. Until you have them, wise decisions are practically impossible. Of course, one of our fears in modern politics is that facts are hard to get at, and so we're left with the superficial. Votes now seem determined by the leader's image, likeability and even the fashion sense of his wife.

But if you think there's a lot at stake during an election, how much more is there in Matthew 28. *Every* political agenda pales in comparison to what is at stake here. For this is not so much a matter of life and death as a matter of life after death. Is such a belief credible?

Now, it's a curious point that nowhere is Jesus' resurrection actually described. The New Testament simply doesn't describe the moment when, after nearly forty-eight hours in a cave, Jesus' heart started to beat again. Instead, we are offered several accounts of its aftermath. That is what we're looking at here – Matthew, Luke and John's different accounts of that momentous Sunday. Each is unique, with its own purpose and narrative style – though of course, the writers are talking about the same events. And this is what makes them so fascinating.

WHEN IT'S TIME FOR A GENERAL ELECTION, A BIG QUESTION TAKES CENTRE STAGE. HOW DO YOU KNOW WHO IS TELLING THE TRUTH?

One of Matthew's key concerns is this issue of witness credibility. No one actually saw Jesus rise. But some pretty weird stuff did happen that first morning. The problem is that there are differing accounts of those events – *both* of which Matthew reports. So who is telling the truth?

Well, before making the judgement call, we must start by getting our facts straight.

## Fact: An Empty Tomb

We start with all the key witnesses present: in verse 1, two women appear, presumably the Marys mentioned in Matthew 27, Mary Magdalene and Mary, the mother of James and Joses. And we know of the soldiers stationed to guard the tomb at the end of Matthew 27. They are all present, and united on one point: the tomb was empty. It's just that their explanations are contradictory.

Matthew, I'm sure, wants us to feel the chills of paranormal activity. It's early in the morning, before the sun's heat had burnt away the dew and cool night air. First there was an earthquake (v. 2) – that's scary enough at the best of times. Then a heavenly figure appeared. What he does next is almost comical. He rolls the tomb cover away and then sits on it, as if to say, 'Job done. Now what do you make of that!' Well, comical if it wasn't so frightening. His appearance in verse 3 is so bright that looking at him is like looking at the sun – in other words, blinding. We're told that this is an angel of the Lord, but the experience of meeting him is similar to what others found on meeting God Himself. Of course, this is not God, but it is clearly someone very close to Him.

**NOTICE THE ANGEL'S FIRST WORDS: 'DO NOT BE AFRAID'. WELL, OF COURSE THEY WERE AFRAID! EVERYONE WAS.**

No wonder everyone present is scared out of their wits:

> 'The guards were so afraid of him that they shook and became like dead men. (v. 4)

Here are hardened Roman soldiers shaking like leaves. Don't dismiss them as cartoon characters – the sorts of morons that Asterix and Obelix had to fight off. No; the point is, these are truly bewildering events.

But whereas the guards are left shaking by the experience, the two Marys get more. Notice the angel's first words: 'Do not be afraid'. Well, of *course* they were afraid! Everyone was. None of this is normal. Which is why these strange events required an explanation.

But the key question is: whose explanation is credible?

# Testimony A: The Women

Now, in the ancient world, the answer to that question was completely obvious. Women? Credible? Certainly not. Ancient Middle Eastern culture didn't really trust women. And Roman law actually discriminated against the testimony of women. They simply weren't credible. Which is why Matthew's account is so countercultural. Women are the first witnesses of the tomb. What's more, they are given instructions from a pretty authoritative source: an angel of the Lord.

> *Do not be afraid, for I know that you are looking for Jesus, who was crucified. He is not here; he has risen, just as he said. Come and see the place where he lay. Then go quickly and tell his disciples: 'He has risen from the dead and is going ahead of you into Galilee. There you will see him.' Now I have told you. (vv. 5–7)*

The reason for the stone being rolled away seems clear now, doesn't it? Not to let Jesus out, but to let the women in, so they could see for themselves. They may not have witnessed Jesus' resurrection itself, but they certainly saw the emptiness of Jesus' grave. Despite the prevailing cultural assumptions, Matthew clearly sees them as credible witnesses – because God did. (And we can see the important role women played in Matthew's story by the fact that a few intriguing women get mentioned in Jesus' family tree back in Matthew 1, which was also pretty unconventional. [1] The angel's explanation for the empty tomb? Jesus has been raised! And He's already left – to go to Galilee.

From now on, everything moves almost too fast. They can't take it in. They are still terrified, but as they obey the angel and leave they are filled with joy (v. 8). Or are they overjoyed but still filled with terror? Who knows? It's all just overwhelming. They can't get their heads around it. But they know there's only one thing for it – to get to the others to tell them about it. Fast.

[1] Matthew 1:1–17 – Tamar (v. 3), Rahab (v. 5), Ruth (v. 5), Uriah's wife, Bathsheba (v. 6), Mary (v. 16)

Which leads to the biggest shock of them all. Four tiny words in verse 9 – four words that seem too puny for the magnitude of what was happening. 'Suddenly Jesus met them.' It's all moving too fast. The last time they saw him was back in chapter 27, where the two Marys, with the other women, saw Him *lifted* onto a cross; they saw Him *dying* on a cross. They saw Him *dead* on a cross. Then, suddenly, Jesus met them.

So not only have these two women been the first to witness the empty tomb, they're the first to meet the risen Lord. And in verse 9 He simply says: 'Greetings.' As someone else might have put it, He had them at 'Hello'. 'They came to him, clasped his feet' and hugged Him. No! That's not what they did. 'They came to him, clasped his feet and worshipped him.' A strange morning just got stranger.

That is not standard practice. But then it's not every day an executed criminal stands right in front of you and says 'Hello'. But notice, He still has to say in verse 10, 'Do not be afraid.' For all their joy, they're still shaking. And they still have a job to do – 'Go and tell my brothers to go to Galilee; there they will see me.'

It's a strange job, though. Why there? Why Galilee? Well, this is Matthew's last chapter. He is deliberately drawing threads together at the end of his book, some of which were introduced right at the start.

And, a search through the gospel for 'Galilee' shows that it is, of course, where Jesus was brought up and spent much time in ministry. But there's more to it. It has prophetic significance too.

**Matthew 4:12–17:** This is right at the start of Jesus' ministry. Jesus lived in Capernaum (4:13) which Matthew tells us has resonance with Isaiah:

> *[for in] Galilee of the Gentiles – the people living in darkness have seen a great light; on those living in the land of the shadow of death a light has dawned.*

**Is it an accident, then, that after the darkest hours of Good Friday, the brightest dawn of Easter should propel the baby church north to Galilee?**

But most wonderfully of all, remember what Jesus said the night He was arrested. **Matthew 26:31,32:**

> *This very night you will all fall away on account of me, for it is written: [in Zech. 13] 'I will strike the shepherd, and the sheep of the flock will be scattered.' But after I have risen, I will go ahead of you into Galilee.*

That explains the angel's comment to the Marys in our passage when he reminded them that Jesus had risen *'as he said'* (my italics). Everyone was bewildered and terrified that first Sunday morning. Who wouldn't be? Matthew stresses the fact. But when the clouds of emotion settled, they would return to the simple point – Jesus had predicted it all! And He said they would meet up again in Galilee.

THE ANGEL TELLS THESE PRIVILEGED WOMEN WHAT EXPLANATION TO GIVE FOR THE EMPTY TOMB: JESUS HAS BEEN RAISED.

There's one other little point around the crucifixion before coming back to our chapter. **Matthew 27:55,56:**

> *Many women were there, watching from a distance. They had followed Jesus from Galilee to care for his needs. Among them were Mary Magdalene, Mary the mother of James and Joses, and the mother of Zebedee's sons.*

Do you see the point? Not only were these women close to Him from the start, Jesus is now saying to His team, after all that has taken place in Jerusalem, 'Let's go home.' As we'll see, it will be just the start of the story. But it's home nonetheless.

So the first witnesses are given their instructions. The angel tells these privileged women what explanation to give for the empty tomb: Jesus has been raised.

Which is very different from the experience of the next group.

## Testimony B: The Soldiers

In verse 11, the women head off in one direction, the guards in another – they now have some pretty uncomfortable explaining to do. But unlike the Marys, their fear is not even remotely tinged with joy. As they went on their way, I'm sure the terrors actually deepened. Guarding a tomb shouldn't have been that tricky, surely? And who will ever believe a story about earthquakes and angels? OK, so we say 'we fell asleep'. But soldiers on guard duty *stay awake. Especially* on the night shift. This does not look good.

The whole paragraph is in fact dripping with irony. Back in Matthew 27, what had been the chief priests' fear? Look at verse 63. They go to Pilate:

> *Sir ... we remember that while he was still alive that deceiver said, 'After three days I will rise again.' So give the order for the tomb to be made secure until the third day. Otherwise, his disciples may come and steal the body and tell the people that he has been raised from the dead. This last deception will be worse than the first.*

'That deceiver', they call Jesus. And they say that the disciples will perpetrate a worse deceit. They're rather concerned about deception, aren't they? So what advice do they have for their guards now?

> *You are to say, 'His disciples came during the night and stole him away while we were asleep.' If this report gets to the governor, we will satisfy him and keep you out of trouble. (28:13,14)*

Who's the great deceiver now? It seems that their chequebooks have greater power than their integrity. For just as they did with Judas, so they now do with the soldiers: they pay them off. And it must have been a lot to make it even vaguely worthwhile for these guards; they were facing a court martial for what had happened.

But again, think back to our original question. In the Roman world, who had greater credibility – a bunch of Jewish mothers, or a small band of imperial troops? No contest. And yet in Matthew's telling of the story, it's no contest either. The women couldn't have found it easy to believe that Jesus was alive, and they were still so full of fears that they could hardly think straight. And yet, they are the ones who simply tell it how it was. The soldiers are the ones who have to make it all up. And according to Matthew 28:15, this is where all the rumours originated:

> *So the soldiers took the money and did as they were instructed. And this story has been widely circulated among the Jews to this very day.*

And actually, not just among the Jews in Matthew's day. Some people today explain away the resurrection like this.

So what do we have so far?

- The angel instructed the women to bear witness: Jesus has been raised
- The priests instructed the soldiers to bear witness: Jesus' body has been stolen

The question is: who has more credibility now?

And so we leave Jerusalem and come at last to Galilee, where it all began.

## Testimony C: All Disciples

Emotions are still running high – how could they not? But notice what happens when they meet at their mountain rendezvous in verse 17: 'When they saw him, they worshipped him; but some doubted.' Just as the Marys' joy was still tinged with fear earlier, so now the worship of the **Eleven** is tinged with doubt.

I'm sure we're not meant to see this as doubt in any rebellious sense, or necessarily as a lack of faith. They would hardly be doing something as crazy as worshipping Him if it was. No; this is Matthew at his down-to-earth best. These events are all too much to take in; how do you even begin to process it and get your head round it? These doubts are more like hesitations and uncertainties – it's all too good to be true. And when things are too good to be true, it is natural to feel a degree of nervousness. But the reason it is so good is because it *is* true … The disciples are just the last in Matthew to catch on to worshipping this Jesus; the wise men did it at His birth; the Marys did it in the garden. Now the disciples do it in Galilee. And notice: they too have their instructions to bear witness – from Jesus Himself.

> **THESE EVENTS ARE ALL TOO MUCH TO TAKE IN; HOW DO YOU EVEN BEGIN TO PROCESS IT AND GET YOUR HEAD ROUND IT?**

So we come to the justly famous 'great commission'. They are some of the most important and weighty words Jesus ever spoke. It could be said that they form His great manifesto, in simplified form, for what God's people would seek to do in His world, as they testify to God's King and build His kingdom. But let us focus on just two key elements, truths which undergird both what the disciples must bear witness to, and indeed, Matthew's whole book.

## (i) Jesus is God's King revealed

> *All authority in heaven and on earth has been given to me. Therefore go and make disciples of all nations … (vv. 18,19)*

Now, what's the big deal with that? Well, think through the whole of Matthew's Gospel. Think back again to Jesus' family tree.[2] One point it makes is that Jesus is a son of David. He has royal blood. And as the opening chapters

[2] Matthew 1:1–17

make clear when the Magi visit the baby, they are looking for the king of the Jews. That was central to His identity.

**But how would this king get people to recognize that identity?** Remember what Satan offered Jesus in the desert?[3] In exchange for worshipping the devil, Jesus could have all the splendour of the kingdoms of the world. So much simpler, so much more painless. Such power ... but at a cost.

Jesus refused. He paid a very different price – at the cross. Instead of the false worship of a despicable liar in order to gain power, He paid the price of obedience to the heavenly Father, in order to show love. And for an even greater reward. As a result, He was granted all authority, not just in the world, but in heaven as well. God the Father was honouring the Son who obeyed Him and not Satan, and raised Him not just to life, but to the highest place.[4]

Jesus is not just king of the Jews – He is King of all nations. And it is on that basis that His first disciples are to make new disciples from every nation. For Jesus is everybody's King, whether they realize it or not. Jesus' assumption in verse 19 is that people will 'go'. The issue is not *whether* they go anywhere, or *where* they go, but *what they do* when they go. For the verse can be translated literally as 'in your going, make disciples'.

But disciples are learners, and learners need teachers. Well, these disciples have no ordinary teacher.

## (ii) Jesus is God revealed

Jesus continues:

> ... *baptising them in the name of the Father and of the Son and of the Holy Spirit, and teaching them to obey everything I have commanded you. And surely I am with you always, to the very end of the age.* (vv. 19,20)

[3] Matthew 4:1–11, especially v. 8  [4] See Philippians 2:5–11

Here are all three members of the Trinity. And that is what a Christian is: someone who is baptized into, and therefore worships, all three. And Matthew has been a gospel particularly concerned with Jesus' teaching – his is the gospel with the Sermon on the Mount, after all. So this is to be passed on. But here is the most astonishing thing: Jesus' parting words and the climax of the whole gospel.

Do you remember what another angel said to reassure Joseph about the baby, back in Matthew 1? He quoted Isaiah and spoke of the virgin who will have a son – and you are to '" . . . call him Immanuel" – which means, God with us' (Matt. 1:23).

It has been a theme of the Bible all the way from Genesis 1. God will live with his people. And here Jesus says, 'I will be with you, My people, always, forever.'

These disciples would not have much credibility in the world's eyes. But they do in the eyes of Jesus. And He commissions them to bear witness – not simply to the fact that He is alive, although He certainly is. But to the truth that He is the divine King who's sticking with us.

**HERE JESUS SAYS, 'I WILL BE WITH YOU, MY PEOPLE, ALWAYS, FOREVER.'**

How do you respond to that? Well, you worship Him even more, don't you? And because of that worship, in fact as part of that worship, we want others to learn from this great teacher, this unique global King, the one true God who is with us.

So it is clear why this is just the start of the story. Galilee is the launch pad for the greatest campaign in human history. To let people know that God in Christ is with us, if only we'd bow to our King, learn from our teacher, and worship our God – Father, Son and Holy Spirit. What's stopping us?

# Matthew 28 in overview

| Matthew 28:1-4 FACT: THE TOMB IS EMPTY | | | |
|---|---|---|---|
| Witnesses are given their instructions | The witness they are to bear | The threads tied up | |
| **28:5-10** | **Angel →** **Women** | JESUS HAS BEEN RAISED! | *Why go to Galilee?* | |
| | **Jesus →** **Women** | | 4:12-16  The light<br>26:32  The Promise<br>27:55  The Start |
| **28:11-15** | **Priests →** **Soldiers** | JESUS' BODY HAS BEEN STOLEN | *Placing a guard on the tomb?*<br>27:63-66  Jesus is 'that deceiver'<br>*But who is the deceiver now?* |
| **28:16-20** | **Jesus →** **Disciples** | JESUS IS WITH US… FOREVER ! | *Jesus the Kind revealed*<br>1:1, 6, 17  Descended from Kind David<br>2:2, 6  Magi search for the King of the Jews<br>4:8,9  Satan offered Him the world's kingdom<br>*Jesus is God with us*<br>1:23  You will call Him 'Immanuel' |

13

# Luke's Account of the Resurrection (Luke 24)

On the first day of the week, very early in the morning, the women took the spices they had prepared and went to the tomb. [2] They found the stone rolled away from the tomb, [3] but when they entered, they did not find the body of the Lord Jesus. [4] While they were wondering about this, suddenly two men in clothes that gleamed like lightning stood beside them. [5] In their fright the women bowed down with their faces to the ground, but the men said to them, 'Why do you look for the living among the dead? [6] He is not here; he has risen! Remember how he told you, while he was still with you in Galilee: [7] "The Son of Man must be delivered into the hands of sinful men, be crucified and on the third day be raised again."' [8] Then they remembered his words.

[9] When they came back from the tomb, they told all these things to the Eleven and to all the others. [10] It was Mary Magdalene, Joanna, Mary the mother of James, and the others with them who told this to the apostles. [11] But they did not believe the women, because their words seemed to them like nonsense. [12] Peter, however, got up and ran to the tomb. Bending over, he saw the strips of linen lying by themselves, and he went away, wondering to himself what had happened.

[13] Now that same day two of them were going to a village called Emmaus, about seven miles from Jerusalem. [14] They were talking with each other about everything that had happened. [15] As they talked and discussed these things with each other, Jesus himself came up and walked along with them;

[16] but they were kept from recognising him.

[17] He asked them, 'What are you discussing together as you walk along?'

They stood still, their faces downcast. [18] One of them, named Cleopas, asked him, 'Are you only a visitor to Jerusalem and do not know the things that have happened there in these days?'

[19] 'What things?' he asked.

'About Jesus of Nazareth,' they replied. 'He was a prophet, powerful in word and deed before God and all the people. [20] The chief priests and our rulers handed him over to be sentenced to death, and they crucified him; [21] but we had hoped that he was the one who was going to redeem Israel. And what is more, it is the third day since all this took place. [22] In addition, some of our women amazed us. They went to the tomb early this morning [23] but didn't find his body. They came and told us that they had seen a vision of angels, who said he was alive. [24] Then some of our companions went to the tomb and found it just as the women had said, but him they did not see.'

[25] He said to them, 'How foolish you are, and how slow of heart to believe all that the prophets have spoken! [26] Did not the Christ have to suffer these things and then enter his glory?' [27] And beginning with Moses and all the Prophets, he explained to them what was said in all the Scriptures concerning himself.

[28] As they approached the village to which they were going, Jesus acted as if he were going further. [29] But they urged him strongly, 'Stay with us, for it is nearly evening; the day is almost over.' So he went in to stay with them.

[30] When he was at the table with them, he took bread,

gave thanks, broke it and began to give it to them. [31] Then their eyes were opened and they recognised him, and he disappeared from their sight. [32] They asked each other, 'Were not our hearts burning within us while he talked with us on the road and opened the Scriptures to us?'

[33] They got up and returned at once to Jerusalem. There they found the Eleven and those with them, assembled together [34] and saying, 'It is true! The Lord has risen and has appeared to Simon.' [35] Then the two told what had happened on the way, and how Jesus was recognised by them when he broke the bread.

[36] While they were still talking about this, Jesus himself stood among them and said to them, 'Peace be with you.'

[37] They were startled and frightened, thinking they saw a ghost. [38] He said to them, 'Why are you troubled, and why do doubts rise in your minds? [39] Look at my hands and my feet. It is I myself! Touch me and see; a ghost does not have flesh and bones, as you see I have.'

[40] When he had said this, he showed them his hands and feet. [41] And while they still did not believe it because of joy and amazement, he asked them, 'Do you have anything here to eat?' [42] They gave him a piece of broiled fish, [43] and he took it and ate it in their presence.

[44] He said to them, 'This is what I told you while I was still with you: Everything must be fulfilled that is written about me in the Law of Moses, the Prophets and the Psalms.'

[45] Then he opened their minds so they could understand the Scriptures. [46] He told them, 'This is

what is written: The Christ will suffer and rise from the dead on the third day, [47] and repentance and forgiveness of sins will be preached in his name to all nations, beginning at Jerusalem. [48] You are witnesses of these things. [49] I am going to send you what my Father has promised; but stay in the city until you have been clothed with power from on high.'

[50] When he had led them out to the vicinity of Bethany, he lifted up his hands and blessed them. [51] While he was blessing them, he left them and was taken up into heaven. [52] Then they worshipped him and returned to Jerusalem with great joy. [53] And they stayed continually at the temple, praising God.

# 2

# The Scriptures Must Be Wonderfully Fulfilled

## Luke's Account of the Resurrection (Luke 24)

Before the last General Election, the spin doctors were out in force on the Thursday night and Friday because of the first-ever Leaders' Debates. 'Their guy' had come out on top, their policies were clarified, theirs the natural party of government. What interested me, though, was not so much what they said, or the interminable post-match analysis. What was intriguing was how the different parties' spin-meisters teed it all up. Various teams lowered expectations for both Cameron and Brown, while nearly everyone was playing Clegg up from the start. He was the one with nothing to lose.

The spin was designed to make it all look planned and expected. 'Everything's under control. Don't worry. We all know what's going to happen.' So when it does happen, we think it's all gone smoothly – even if their guy was considered to have lost the debate. That's one of the things about prediction. It gives you authority . . . if, and only if, it comes true.

Of course, the predictions for the election were not especially surprising. It was all a matter of spin. Anyone with even the remotest understanding of British politics could have made a reasonable stab. But if I predicted that the Monster Raving Loony Party would be the party of power in the next Parliament, you would rightly think that absurd.

And yet to some minds, this is no different from the suggestion that Jesus would come back from the dead. How ridiculous, predicted or not! Well, Luke is at pains in his account of Jesus' resurrection to show that it is not ridiculous. If Matthew, in his account, had been concerned for the credibility of the witnesses, Luke is focused on the credibility of the evidence.

Let's see how the whole chapter hangs together, and how Luke wraps up the whole book. To do that, we must remember why Luke wrote in the first place. Having sifted through the various eyewitness accounts, he writes at the very start, in verse 4: 'so that you may know the certainty of the things you have been taught.'

IF MATTHEW, IN HIS ACCOUNT, HAD BEEN CONCERNED FOR THE CREDIBILITY OF THE WITNESSES, LUKE IS FOCUSED ON THE CREDIBILITY OF THE EVIDENCE.

Surprising though it may seem, faith, as far as the New Testament is concerned, is always rational – and for Luke, it is based on certainty. It is not wishful thinking (even if what we might wish for actually coincides with what we have faith in). So let's see how. As we would expect from someone who's gathered eyewitness testimonies, it's vivid and lively – and all the more so because it's set in three very different places. But each time, he's growing our certainty about its truth – even though believing that a dead man has come to life seems absurd. But in each scene, the witnesses move from perplexity to faith as a result of proof and predictions.

# 1. Frightened in the Garden (24:1–12)

As with Matthew, we have the same women coming to the garden early in the morning. And again, they find the tomb empty. The eagle-eyed will have noticed that Luke mentions two angelic figures (in v. 4), whereas Matthew 28 only mentions one.[5] At the very least, it proves they have been using independent sources. But note also, there is no inherent contradiction – it's just a matter of how you describe it. You can either mention that there are two, as Luke does, or merely highlight the one who speaks, perhaps as an angelic spokesman, as Matthew does. Either way, the women react in the same way.

• **Perplexity**

> *In their fright the women bowed down with their faces to the ground... (v. 5)*

Their perplexity is profound, but understandable. Not just because the tomb is empty, no doubt, but because it's no small thing to be confronted by heaven. It's terrifying. It's easy to look down our noses and draw quick conclusions about the first disciples. We pick up what the angelic figures say in verse 5: 'Why do you look for the living among the dead?' And we wonder: Why didn't they get it? Why didn't they remember what Jesus had taught? Why didn't they believe that Jesus really was alive?

**WHY DIDN'T THEY GET IT? WHY DIDN'T THEY REMEMBER WHAT JESUS HAD TAUGHT? WHY DIDN'T THEY BELIEVE THAT JESUS REALLY WAS ALIVE?**

They're easy questions. But this was a staggering situation. Don't forget: the emotional roller-coaster of the previous week had been overwhelming, which is why the angel's words are so important. For what dissolves their perplexity is Jesus' prediction.

• **Predictions**

Look at them again:

> *Why do you look for the living among the dead? He is not here; he has risen! Remember how he told you, while he was*

---

[5] For a scholarly but very readable analysis of how the gospel's different resurrection narratives are compatible, see John Wenham's brilliant *Easter Enigma* (Eugene, OR: Wipf and Stock Publishers, 2005).

*still with you in Galilee... (vv. 5,6)*

Then, unlike Matthew, Luke makes it explicit:

*The Son of Man must be delivered into the hands of sinful men, be crucified and on the third day be raised again. Then they remembered his words. (vv. 7,8)*

So what words did they remember, exactly? Let's retrace the journey Luke's Gospel has taken us on. For there are in fact two main occasions when Jesus predicts His death in Luke – and it's interesting to see when they come.

### • Before the journey's start (Luke 9:22)

This is the occasion, familiar to readers of Mark's Gospel. We're up in Galilee, near Caesarea Philippi where Peter first voiced his recognition that Jesus was the king (#1 on the map[6]). You are the Christ, he says. Then Jesus makes His prediction:

*The Son of Man must suffer many things and [must] be rejected by the elders, chief priests and teachers of the law, and he must be killed and on the third day [must] be raised to life.*

They are strange words – and the strangest is that little word 'must'. I confess I added in two 'musts' of my own to the translation, but that is completely legitimate. He is saying it *must* happen. Now, neither Jesus nor Luke tell us *why* it was necessary – yet. Only that it was. Then very soon after this, Luke shows how Jesus got the ball rolling for fulfilment of this prediction. Look at 9:51:

*As the time approached for him to be taken up to heaven, Jesus resolutely set out for Jerusalem.*

Notice Jesus' goal here: it's not the cross, or even the resurrection. It's the ascension. That's where this is all heading. And what does Jesus do to start? He sets out for Jerusalem. For that is where everything will take place, at incalculable personal cost.

[5] The base map is taken from the ESV study bible (www.esvstudybible.org)

So everything that occurs after Luke 9:52 takes place on that inexorable journey south.

Then where does Jesus' second prediction happen?

### Before the journey's end (Luke 18:31–34)

*We are going up to Jerusalem, and everything that is written by the prophets about the Son of Man will be fulfilled. He will be handed over to the Gentiles. They will mock him, insult him, spit on him, flog him and kill him. On the third day he will rise again.<end indent>*

Now we get an idea of why Jesus said 'must' the first time – it's to fulfil what the prophets wrote. What is added is the involvement of the Gentiles, plus the mocking and torture. But still – on the third day, He will rise again.

But look how they responded, in verse 34:

*The disciples did not understand any of this. Its meaning was hidden from them, and they did not know what he was talking about.*

Its meaning was concealed, presumably, both because it was too much to get their heads around, and because the time was not yet right for them to 'get it'. But look where we are. (#2 on the map). Just into the next chapter, Luke 19, we have the Triumphal Entry into Jerusalem, the royal capital. Jesus' predictions are bookends for His journey – His journey to the very place where it will all occur.

**JESUS' PREDICTIONS ARE BOOKENDS FOR HIS JOURNEY – HIS JOURNEY TO THE VERY PLACE WHERE IT WILL ALL OCCUR.**

And now that it has happened, Easter Sunday is the time when it all begins to make sense. And these women are the first to find out. And as it clicks into place, no wonder they are then desperate to tell the others, in Luke 24. They run to them. But the reaction they got was the reaction of confusion and grief in 24:11:

*But they did not believe the women, because their words*

*seemed to them like nonsense.*

Of course, that didn't stop Peter going to have a look for himself. And what did he find? Well, he too had to confirm what proof the women had found:

### • Proof

*Bending over, he saw the strips of linen lying by themselves, and he went away, wondering to himself what had happened. (24:12)*

Unlikely as it had first seemed, Peter could see for himself. The tomb was indeed empty. The linen bandages were all there. He certainly had a lot to wonder to himself about. It's clear that the perplexity of the day hasn't disappeared. It is still troubling and strange.

But we have seen how for the women at least, their encounter with the angelic figures has begun to break through their fears. They have seen the proof of the empty tomb and they have been reminded of Jesus' own predictions.

Why does this matter?

Well, it is not a matter of political spin doctors trying to give the impression of being in control and knowing what's going to happen. Anyone can do that within a range of predictable outcomes. It's just a matter of educated guesswork. But this – **this is utterly different. What happened here was a prediction of the utterly *unpredictable*.** This is not normal. To predict something like this suggests you are actually *behind* something like this. And who can possibly be behind dying and then rising on the third day?

But before we ponder too long on that, we're whisked away to a road outside Jerusalem.

## 2. Irritated on the Road (24:13–35)

Here we have two friends of Jesus; we discover in verse 18 that one is called Cleopas. It's the only time he is mentioned in the New Testament. But whereas the women met angels, these two meet Jesus Himself, although in verse 16 they are kept from recognizing Him. Surprisingly, they still seem unready to come to terms with the truth. Something's missing. So what is it?

Well, first of all, their perplexity is clear.

### • Perplexity

I'm sure you've had those moments where you've got a lot on your mind and you just need time to think. Perhaps there's something stressful at work, and you're sitting on the train after a long day; the last thing you want is a complete stranger to start chatting. It's especially annoying because you'd worked so hard at the 'leave-me-alone' body language. You know: arms crossed, legs crossed, fingers crossed and even eyes crossed. What else does a guy have to do to get some peace?

Well, these two were like that as they walked. The etiquette of travelling in the ancient world wasn't like it is on British trains, where you keep yourself to yourself. You had to have a reason not to talk with others on the road. But in verse 17 they are downcast – and then you can hear Cleopas' irritation in verse 18:

> Are you the only visitor to Jerusalem and do not know the things that have happened there in these days?

Oh, the ironies of that question! Jesus had indeed visited Jerusalem, and been at the very centre of all that happened there. But He is gentle and patient. 'What things?' he asks (v. 19).

What is fascinating about their reply is that they've got all their facts right – Jesus, a prophet, 'powerful in word and deed'. They even echo Jesus very own predictions in verse 20:

> The chief priests and our rulers handed him over to be sentenced to death, and they crucified him

Sounds like what we've already quoted. Even more bizarrely, they acknowledge in verse 21 that it's the third day, and they've even heard about what the women and

Peter had found - angels and an empty tomb (vv. 22–24).

And yet, despite it all – what are they doing? They're leaving Jerusalem! Why? The telltale verse in 21:

> *we had hoped that he was the one who was going to redeem Israel.*

But of course he wasn't. That's the implication. Why else leave? They've got the facts straight; but it seems that it is not just Jesus' identity they fail to see. They fail to get the whole thing. So now perhaps we see why they were kept from seeing Him. So, after biding His time, Jesus can now get to work. And He pulls no punches.

### • Predictions

You're foolish and you're slow! Why? You should have believed . . .

> *. . . all that the prophets have spoken! Did not the Christ have to suffer these things and then enter his glory? And beginning with Moses and all the Prophets, he explained to them what was said in all the Scriptures concerning himself. (vv. 25–27)*

He had to suffer – because He was predicted to suffer! He had to rise – because He was predicted to rise! These two had the facts; they just hadn't pieced them together with God's interpretation of the facts – one that He'd given centuries in advance. 'Moses' is shorthand for the Pentateuch, the first five books of the Old Testament; 'the Prophets' shorthand for all the rest. The point: it had all been predicted.

> HE HAD TO SUFFER – BECAUSE HE WAS PREDICTED TO SUFFER! HE HAD TO RISE – BECAUSE HE WAS PREDICTED TO RISE!

And then comes the...

### •Proof

Their initial frostiness has completely evaporated, and now they want to stay with Jesus on the journey. They stop for supper at a nearby pub or somewhere, and they eat together. As soon as they finally do recognise Him – yes, it is Him! He's alive! He's with us – as soon as they do, He disappears! But they've had proof of His vitality. He had definitely been with them and they had eaten together. And what do they remember – verse 32:

> Were not our hearts burning within us while he talked with us on the road and opened the Scriptures to us?

You see, it's not simply that this was the most incredible Bible study in history; it's that it all makes sense now. Their perplexity is dispelled, and the risen Jesus gives them proof and explains the fulfilment of Old Testament predictions. And so they turn around, and do exactly what the women did in the morning. Go back to tell the others. What they find is that Jesus had beaten them to it, which makes our final stop a final surprise. Because you might have thought they would have come to terms with it all by now.

# 3. Startled in the Upper Room (24:33–49)

## • Perplexity

It's rather comical; I wonder if the Lord Jesus could see the funny side in it all. In verse 36, they're actually talking about Jesus being alive, and then when Jesus suddenly appears and says 'Shalom! Peace!' they jump out of their skins thinking they've seen a ghost. They are still perplexed!

## • Proof

So Jesus does what He can to prove their understandable first assumptions wrong.

- He tells them to look closely and to touch Him (v. 39) – you can't do that to a ghost;
- He asks them to give Him something to eat (v. 41) – you can't expect a ghost to do that!

And yet even now it's all too much. Look in verse 41: they still did not believe it because of 'joy and amazement'. I love it! So real.

Which leads to Jesus teaching them again. And His theme is the same – told you about all this, and the Scriptures told you about all this.

### • Prediction

> *This is what I told you while I was still with you: Everything must be fulfilled that is written about me in the Law of Moses, the Prophets and the Psalms [being shorthand for wisdom literature]. (v 44)*

Is it sounding familiar yet? But in case you're wondering why it's taken them so long, the key to it all comes in verse 45: Jesus opens their minds to understand. They need Him to unlock their minds and dispel the fog.

So hopefully we've got clear that all the events of this unique weekend in world history were planned, predicted and prepared for. The unpredictable had been predicted. But so what? Jesus was special; what more does it prove?

THE UNPREDICTABLE HAD BEEN PREDICTED. BUT SO WHAT? JESUS WAS SPECIAL; WHAT MORE DOES IT PROVE?

Well, suppose I get run over by a bus. I hope very much that I'd be missed. But suppose then a few days later I suddenly come back to life and walk out of the mortuary. You'd be impressed. But you wouldn't suddenly conclude, 'Ah, that Mark Meynell – he's God!' Certainly not.

But suppose for the last three years I'd been going around saying that this is exactly what would happen. That would change things. You'd then start raking over everything else I'd said. Now suppose I'd said that my death and resurrection would actually achieve something? Now that it had happened you'd gradually, or perhaps very quickly, put all the jigsaw pieces together.

Which is exactly what happened with Jesus' disciples. He said that now they were in a position to do what He'd predicted for them. To bear witness – for now

> repentance and forgiveness of sins will be preached ... to all nations, beginning at Jerusalem. (v. 47)

That's what it achieved. Jesus has won, and now we have hope. And everyone in the world needs to hear about it.

As the chapter has proceeded, the picture has become clearer and clearer; the early morning mists are being burned off by the Son of God Himself, and as people get it, their natural instinct is to tell it. They will get power to be witnesses, as Jesus says in verse 49 – but that, like the final verses about His ascension, is the story of Luke's sequel, the book of Acts.

**JESUS HAS WON, AND NOW WE HAVE HOPE. AND EVERYONE IN THE WORLD NEEDS TO HEAR ABOUT IT.**

Luke set out to give us *the certainty of the things you have been taught.* (1:4)

But he has done far more. He has given us hope, and he has given us understanding.

# Luke 24 in overview

Luke wrote his gospel... *So that you may know the certainty of the things you have been taught* (Luke 1:4)

Who was where? The disciples' *Perplexity* replaced... ...by the *certainty* of the things they'd been taught

## Frightened in the Garden (224:1-12)

**• The women**
(*Mary Magdalene, Joanna, Mary mother of James et al*)

**• Peter**

**Surprise visitors:**
*Two men gleaming like lightening*

**Perplexity**
• 24:5 Fear and awe
• 24:12 wondering to himself

**Predictions** 'just as he told you'
The bookends of Jesus' journey:
• Luke 9:22 (*the start of the Jerusalem journey – Luke 9:51*)
• Luke 18:31-33 (*the end of the Jerusalem journey – Luke 19:28*)
*Note: Luke 18:34 – the disciples didn't understand*

**Proof**
• Luke 24:12 Peter sees the strips of linen: the tomb is EMPTY

## Irritated on the Road (24:13:35)

**• Cleopas and friend**

**Surprise visitor:**
*Jesus himself but disguised!*

**Perplexity**
• 24:18 irritated
• 24:2 If despairing and confused
• 24:32 thrilled

They are kept from recognising Him, but are stupid and slow!

**Predictions** 'Christ MUST suffer...'
• Luke 24: Moses and all the Prophets concerning HIMSELF

**Proof**
• Luke 24:32 – He was with us, shared bread, our hearts burned

## Startled in the Upper Room (24:33-49)

**• Cleopas and friend**

**• Eleven + others**
(e.g. the women?)

**Surprise visitor:**
*Jesus Himself suddenly appears!*

**Perplexity**
• 24:37 startled and frightened
• 24:41 can't believe it because of joy and amazement

**Proof**
• Luke 24:39 look and touch: can't do that with ghosts!
• Luke 24:41-43 Eating fish: ghosts can't do that!

**Predictions**
• Luke 24:44 I told you when with you
• Luke 24:46,47 Everything in OT MUST be fulfilled
*SO... go to city until you receive power to be witnesses*

From Mountain to Temple (24:50-53) Jesus taken up into heaven – a trailer for the sequel; THE BOOK OF ACTS!

# John's Account of the Resurrection (John 20 – 21)

20:1 Early on the first day of the week, while it was still dark, Mary Magdalene went to the tomb and saw that the stone had been removed from the entrance. 2 So she came running to Simon Peter and the other disciple, the one Jesus loved, and said, 'They have taken the Lord out of the tomb, and we don't know where they have put him!'

3 So Peter and the other disciple started for the tomb. 4 Both were running, but the other disciple outran Peter and reached the tomb first. 5 He bent over and looked in at the strips of linen lying there but did not go in. 6 Then Simon Peter, who was behind him, arrived and went into the tomb. He saw the strips of linen lying there, 7 as well as the burial cloth that had been around Jesus' head. The cloth was folded up by itself, separate from the linen. 8 Finally the other disciple, who had reached the tomb first, also went inside. He saw and believed. 9 (They still did not understand from Scripture that Jesus had to rise from the dead.)

10 Then the disciples went back to their homes, 11 but Mary stood outside the tomb crying. As she wept, she bent over to look into the tomb 12 and saw two angels in white, seated where Jesus' body had been, one at the head and the other at the foot.

13 They asked her, 'Woman, why are you crying?'

'They have taken my Lord away,' she said, 'and I don't know where they have put him.' 14 At this, she turned round and saw Jesus standing there, but she did not realise that it was Jesus.

¹⁵ 'Woman,' he said, 'why are you crying? Who is it you are looking for?'

Thinking he was the gardener, she said, 'Sir, if you have carried him away, tell me where you have put him, and I will get him.'

¹⁶ Jesus said to her, 'Mary.'

She turned towards him and cried out in Aramaic, 'Rabboni!' (which means Teacher).

¹⁷ Jesus said, 'Do not hold on to me, for I have not yet returned to the Father. Go instead to my brothers and tell them, "I am returning to my Father and your Father, to my God and your God."'

¹⁸ Mary Magdalene went to the disciples with the news: 'I have seen the Lord!' And she told them that he had said these things to her.

¹⁹ On the evening of that first day of the week, when the disciples were together, with the doors locked for fear of the Jews, Jesus came and stood among them and said, 'Peace be with you!' ²⁰ After he said this, he showed them his hands and side. The disciples were overjoyed when they saw the Lord.

²¹ Again Jesus said, 'Peace be with you! As the Father has sent me, I am sending you.' ²² And with that he breathed on them and said, 'Receive the Holy Spirit. ²³ If you forgive anyone his sins, they are forgiven; if you do not forgive them, they are not forgiven.'

²⁴ Now Thomas (called Didymus), one of the Twelve, was not with the disciples when Jesus came. ²⁵ So the other disciples told him, 'We have seen the Lord!'

But he said to them, 'Unless I see the nail marks in his hands and put my finger where the nails were, and put my hand into his side, I will not believe it.'

²⁶ A week later his disciples were in the house again,

and Thomas was with them. Though the doors were locked, Jesus came and stood among them and said, 'Peace be with you!' [27] Then he said to Thomas, 'Put your finger here; see my hands. Reach out your hand and put it into my side. Stop doubting and believe.'

[28] Thomas said to him, 'My Lord and my God!'

[29] Then Jesus told him, 'Because you have seen me, you have believed; blessed are those who have not seen and yet have believed.'

[30] Jesus did many other miraculous signs in the presence of his disciples, which are not recorded in this book. 31 But these are written that you may believe that Jesus is the Christ, the Son of God, and that by believing you may have life in his name.

[21:1] Afterwards Jesus appeared again to his disciples, by the Sea of Tiberias. It happened this way: [2] Simon Peter, Thomas (called Didymus), Nathanael from Cana in Galilee, the sons of Zebedee, and two other disciples were together. [3] "I'm going out to fish," Simon Peter told them, and they said, "We'll go with you." So they went out and got into the boat, but that night they caught nothing. [4] Early in the morning, Jesus stood on the shore, but the disciples did not realize that it was Jesus. [5] He called out to them, "Friends, haven't you any fish?" "No," they answered. [6] He said, "Throw your net on the right side of the boat and you will find some." When they did, they were unable to haul the net in because of the large number of fish.

[7] Then the disciple whom Jesus loved said to Peter, "It is the Lord!" As soon as Simon Peter heard him say, "It is the Lord," he wrapped his outer garment around him (for he had taken it off) and jumped into the water. [8] The other disciples followed in the boat,

towing the net full of fish, for they were not far from shore, about a hundred yards. ⁹ When they landed, they saw a fire of burning coals there with fish on it, and some bread. ¹⁰ Jesus said to them, "Bring some of the fish you have just caught."

¹¹ Simon Peter climbed aboard and dragged the net ashore. It was full of large fish, 153, but even with so many the net was not torn. ¹² Jesus said to them, "Come and have breakfast." None of the disciples dared ask him, "Who are you?" They knew it was the Lord. ¹³ Jesus came, took the bread and gave it to them, and did the same with the fish. ¹⁴ This was now the third time Jesus appeared to his disciples after he was raised from the dead.

¹⁵ When they had finished eating, Jesus said to Simon Peter, "Simon son of John, do you truly love me more than these?" "Yes, Lord," he said, "you know that I love you." Jesus said, "Feed my lambs."

¹⁶ Again Jesus said, "Simon son of John, do you truly love me?" He answered, "Yes, Lord, you know that I love you." Jesus said, "Take care of my sheep."

¹⁷ The third time he said to him, "Simon son of John, do you love me?"

Peter was hurt because Jesus asked him the third time, "Do you love me?" He said, "Lord, you know all things; you know that I love you." Jesus said, "Feed my sheep. ¹⁸ I tell you the truth, when you were younger you dressed yourself and went where you wanted; but when you are old you will stretch out your hands, and someone else will dress you and lead you where you do not want to go." ¹⁹ Jesus said this to indicate the kind of death by which Peter would glorify God. Then he said to him, "Follow me!"

<sup>20</sup> Peter turned and saw that the disciple whom Jesus loved was following them. (This was the one who had leaned back against Jesus at the supper and had said, "Lord, who is going to betray you?") <sup>21</sup> When Peter saw him, he asked, "Lord, what about him?"

<sup>22</sup> Jesus answered, "If I want him to remain alive until I return, what is that to you? You must follow me." <sup>23</sup> Because of this, the rumor spread among the brothers that this disciple would not die. But Jesus did not say that he would not die; he only said, "If I want him to remain alive until I return, what is that to you?"

<sup>24</sup> This is the disciple who testifies to these things and who wrote them down. We know that his testimony is true.

<sup>25</sup> Jesus did many other things as well. If every one of them were written down, I suppose that even the whole world would not have room for the books that would be written.

# 3

# Revolutionary Encounters with the Risen Christ

John's Account of the Resurrection
(John 20 –21)

I'd never heard of Sir Tim Hunt until the other night, but that's only because I don't know a great deal about scientific research. I didn't catch the whole programme, but the biochemist was profiled in the BBC4 series *Beautiful Minds*. In 2001 he was awarded, with two colleagues, the Nobel Prize for Medicine, because of his discovery of the protein cyclin which is apparently a crucial ingredient in cell division. My inability to explain it didn't stop me being swept up by his excitement at discovering it in 1982. He'd done a simple experiment, but the results were very striking, with a clear, fixed pattern emerging. He immediately knew this was important, but he didn't really know what it all meant. He had his suspicions, but he had to check it with someone he could trust. That night at a drinks party he bumped into a mentor, John Gerhardt, and remembers deliberately brushing someone off who just wanted to chit-chat. This talk was way too important for social niceties. He said, 'This was the most exciting scientific conversation of my entire life, bar none.' It changed his life. There was still a lot of work to do, but that moment changed everything.

What we find in John's closing chapters is something similar – an amazing discovery that didn't completely make sense, until some private conversations changed everything. The difference is that they weren't conversations with a special mentor, but with the one who defeated death. But the best thing about it is that unlike Tim Hunt's cocktail party friend, we don't get brushed off. We get to eavesdrop on these intensely private but very special moments.

John starts his resurrection account in exactly the same place as the other three Gospels – with the empty tomb. And even though his description is different, it is fascinating to see the same people involved: Mary Magdalene and Peter, who we now discover is with the so-called 'disciple . . . Jesus loved' (vv. 2,7,20). And as we see from the very end of the book, this is John, the writer of the Gospel, himself. So we are reading the first-hand account of an eyewitness.

Mary, Peter and John all discover the tomb empty and, more significantly, in verse 7, the burial cloth is folded. Presumably, the reason is they're no longer required. The one buried in them won't be returning to the grave.

**JOHN, 'THE OTHER DISCIPLE', GOES IN AND PUTS TWO AND TWO TOGETHER IMMEDIATELY. HE SAW AND BELIEVED.**

Now we see that John, 'the other disciple' in verse 8, goes in and puts two and two together immediately. He saw and believed. Interestingly, in verse 9 we're told that neither he nor Peter understood 'from Scripture that Jesus had to rise from the dead' – Jesus still had work to do to explain that, as we saw in Luke 24.

But what John does is very important. He sees and believes. And his own experience mirrors precisely what he longs for his readers to experience, with one difference – we can't see what he saw. We must rely on eyewitnesses.

> Jesus did many other miraculous signs in the presence of his disciples, which are not recorded in this book. But these are written that you may believe that Jesus is the Christ, the Son of God, and that by believing you may have life in his name. (vv. 30,31)

This sums up his purpose in writing the whole Gospel. But

it also sums up what is going on in these last two chapters. For after all that has happened, and all that Jesus has taught, we find that Jesus has conversations with three very different people, each with their own turmoil, questions and history, each of them old friends, each fully aware of the discovery of the empty tomb. But none has yet fully grasped its implications for them personally. For that, they need a conversation with Jesus.

# 1. Jesus reunited with a grieving friend: Mary

Mary Magdalene got there first, and she'll always be remembered for that. All four Gospels make a point of saying so. And she finds the tomb empty, but then goes back to find the others. Her one conclusion (in v. 2):

> *They have taken the Lord out of the tomb, and we don't know where they have put him!*

So for whatever reason, she has not drawn the same conclusions that John does in verse 8. Instead she naturally assumes the body's been stolen. But there's still this niggling feeling; something doesn't quite add up. Just as Peter and John are going back home, Mary can't resist one more look. So she returns to the tomb. She meets the angelic figures Luke talked about. She repeats her conclusion about the stolen body. So far, so good. But then things take a dramatic turn.

In Luke 24, Jesus appeared incognito to the two on the Emmaus road. Now Jesus appears incognito to Mary. It's quite ironic, really. In verse 13 she says, 'I don't know where they have put him.' And then immediately we realize no one's put him anywhere, because 'At this, she turned round and saw Jesus standing there, but she did not realise that it was Jesus' (v. 14).

And Jesus puts the same question to her as the angels. It

strikes me that the tone is very similar to His tone with the two going to Emmaus. He gently probes. '. . . why are you crying? Who is it you are looking for?' (v. 15) All very measured. But like the Emmaus pair, Mary doesn't get the hint. So she asks this stranger the same question: 'Where have you put him?' But she assumes that He is the gardener. Now, is that an accident? Of course, a gardener is precisely the sort of person you'd expect to meet in a garden. But this is John's Gospel, and John loves double meanings and allusions. He has deliberately echoed the book of Genesis already, with his prologue echoing the creation accounts – 'In the beginning was the Word' (John 1:1). Could we now be in a place of another new beginning, with God creating life in a garden? Who knows? We can only speculate.

But the wonderful and deeply touching thing is that the trigger for clearing Mary's blindness is just one word from the 'gardener', in verse 16. Her name. Mary.

That's enough. Just her name.

I went to the sorts of schools where it was strictly surnames only. It explains a lot, I'm sure – as my so-called friends are quick to point out! It was certainly how teachers referred to us, and I guess that rubbed off, so kids did it too. But I vividly remember the moment when I was chatting with one teacher – one of those teachers you hugely respect but are not a little scared of. I've no idea what we were talking about. But I do remember that he suddenly called me 'Mark'. You could have knocked me down with a feather. It hadn't occurred to me that he even knew my first name.

And it meant a lot. Knowing someone's name is important. **Being on first-name terms is a genuine sign of friendship. And Mary was a real friend of Jesus.** She was the only person recorded in the Gospels as present at Jesus' crucifixion, His burial and His empty tomb. The only one. She was clearly devoted to Him, and with good reason. We know very little about her background; she is almost certainly not the so-called sinful woman who anointed

Jesus with her tears (Luke 7:36–50). But we do know from Luke 8 that Jesus had healed her of some nasty affliction, which entailed having seven demons cast out of her. We also learn there that she was quite wealthy, and so with two others mentioned (Joanna and Susanna) was able to support Jesus and the disciples financially (8:2,3). She'd been there from the beginning and was absolutely devoted to Jesus.

So no wonder she clings to him. Now that He's back, she can't face the thought of letting her rabbi, and above all, her friend, go. He changed her life when she had been utterly helpless and at the mercy of demonic forces. She'd lost Jesus once; she didn't want to lose Him again.

But this is the fog of emotions talking, because she will *never* lose Jesus again. Not now – not after He has defeated death. So Jesus says, in verse 17:

> *Do not hold on to me, for I have not yet returned to the Father.*

In other words, Jesus is saying, 'I've still got work to do. This is not the end. In fact, it is just the beginning.'

> *Go instead to my brothers and tell them, 'I am returning to my Father and your Father, to my God and your God.'*

Now Jesus is saying, 'You've got work to do, too. Tell them.' But notice what she is to say. This time it's not simply that He's alive. She is to tell them that He is passing through – He's on His way back to the Father's presence; no small thing after the agony of the crucifixion, when He was barred from the Father. But notice, He is not just Jesus' Father and God. Jesus tells Mary that He is *her* Father and God too. This relationship is personal. And it's all because of Jesus. Remember that – because she will not be the only one. But

**GO INSTEAD TO MY BROTHERS AND TELL THEM, 'I AM RETURNING TO MY FATHER AND YOUR FATHER, TO MY GOD AND YOUR GOD.'**

as she leaves, and as Jesus passes from her presence, she is looking to the future.

So she goes to tell them. 'I have seen the Lord!' she says (v. 18). Now, when she says 'Lord' there, she could simply be saying Master - *kurios* is the Greek word, and it is the sort of word a shop assistant might use to be polite to a customer. It just means 'Sir'. It's a simple term of respect. And I'm sure that was how the disciples understood it throughout their years with Jesus – until it gradually dawned on them that it meant much more . . . at the same time. As we'll see.

**HE, THE GOD OF COMPASSION, COMES ALONGSIDE US IN OUR GRIEF – GENTLY BUT FULL OF HOPE, BECAUSE HE IS FULL OF LIFE.**

But we have seen how tenderly Jesus comes alongside a grieving friend. And we see how He, the God of compassion, comes alongside us in our grief – gently but full of hope, because He is full of life. He has defeated the grave, with the result that now, in Christ, we grieve for sure, but not as those without hope.[7]

## 2. Jesus reunited with an honest sceptic: Thomas

That night, the disciples are in the upper room. They're confused, uncertain and scared. And just as we saw in Luke 24, Jesus appears – presumably He has already visited the Emmaus road by this point. He says those wonderful words: 'Peace be with you!' (v. 19) *Shalom*. It's such a rich concept – for it means peace in the sense of end of hostilities and fighting. But it is much, much more; it is peace in the sense of total well-being and welfare. It means *all* is well. And when He shows His hands and side (v. 20), the disciples are overjoyed. They, like Mary, have 'seen the Lord'.

[7] 1 Thessalonians 4:13

Then comes a strange moment. Jesus seems to give them an acted parable of what will happen in a few weeks at Pentecost. He breathes and tells them they will receive the Holy Spirit. But it is a foretaste of the job they themselves will have to do. They too are looking to the future. They are to bring the good news of forgiveness to all who will hear it.

But there was a slight snag. Did you spot it in verse 24? Thomas wasn't there. Poor chap. The others are full of it, but he completely missed it: 'We've seen the Lord.'

What he says in verse 25 is perfectly reasonable. He's got a bad rap as Doubting Thomas – which of course gives great encouragement to fellow doubters – but it is probably a little unfair to him. We can understand what he asks for:

> *Unless I see the nail marks in his hands and put my finger where the nails were, and put my hand into his side, I will not believe it.*

But think about it – he's only asking for what the other disciples had. He missed out on Jesus' visit – it was only fair. He knew about the discoveries of the empty tomb; he heard what the others had experienced. But he just couldn't be sure what it all meant. His is a reasonable scepticism, but it is scepticism nonetheless. And the truth is that we are all in pretty much the same boat as he was. We don't get to see the nail marks for ourselves, either. So how do we cope with that?

Poor old Thomas; in verse 26 we see that he has to wait a whole week. Can you imagine? All the others are still full of it. And he's got to sit tight. Who knows what that must have been like?

But just as Jesus wonderfully and patiently came alongside the grieving Mary, He eventually comes to Thomas:

> *Shalom… Put your finger here; see my hands. Reach out your hand and put it into my side. Stop doubting and believe. (vv. 26,27)*

That's exactly what he asked for. Jesus clearly knows what

His disciples have been talking about in His absence. He knows Thomas, as well. And He understands his doubts and scepticism. But notice – He's actually stronger at the end than you might think. He literally says: *'Don't be an unbeliever. Be a believer.'*

Don't dismiss scepticism. Jesus doesn't. It's important; it stops people being conned and gullible. Tim Keller helpfully puts it like this:

> *A faith without some doubts is like a human body without any antibodies in it. People who blithely go through life too busy or indifferent to ask hard questions about why they believe as they do will find themselves defenceless against either the experience of tragedy or the probing questions of a smart sceptic.*[8]

But now that Jesus has appeared, it is time to put that scepticism aside, which is precisely what Thomas does. And notice: he doesn't blink. He doesn't even need to touch Jesus' wounds. Just as John did earlier, Thomas *saw and believed*. And in verse 28 he comes out with the most momentous words ever uttered:

> *My Lord and my God!*

Do you see the echo of what Jesus said to Mary? But by now Lord, *kurios* has gained far deeper significance. This is now clearly the Old Testament name of God. Lord – Adonai. In case there's doubt about that, Thomas reinforces it when He calls Jesus God. But the most wonderful thing is that this sceptic truly has gone from unbeliever to believer. For he says *my* Lord and *my* God.

Now I confess a sneaking jealousy of Thomas. I wish I'd had the same conversation. It would make life so much easier. But Jesus is a step ahead of me. For He knows that most of us will not share Thomas' experience. But we can still be blessed:

[8] Timothy Keller, *The Reason for God* (New York: Dutton, 2008), p. xvi.

> *Because you have seen me, you have believed; blessed are those who have not seen and yet have believed. (v. 29)*

It is still possible to believe what John, Mary and Thomas all believed. In some ways, Jesus is calling on all these eyewitnesses to help those of us who have not seen – Jesus is indeed the Christ everyone has been waiting for. And such a belief is not an intellectual assent to an idea, it is a revolutionary truth that transforms everything – one's priorities, one's worship, one's life, and above all, one's future. For why did John record what the eyewitnesses had seen in his book? Verse 31 tells us:

> *that you may believe that Jesus is the Christ, the Son of God, and that by believing you may have life in his name.*

Jesus is alive, and so all who trust in Him are bound to Him so deeply that we thereby share His life. Forever.

So Thomas was effectively given a job, too – to help those who have not seen. The implication is that it is possible to believe this without having seen, and regardless of how sceptical we might be. This stands up to scrutiny; sometimes, *intense* scrutiny. Even the most hostile of sceptics come to the conclusion that Jesus really is this Christ.

John is a great one for tying up loose ends. And you might think that chapter 21 is an afterthought. After all, he acknowledged in verse 30 that Jesus did too many other miraculous signs to include. So why do we get this amazing catch of 153 fish? Well, it reinforces the reality and wonder of Jesus' resurrection life. But more importantly, it sets the scene for one final conversation. For there is one huge loose end hanging. It's a big one. Because Simon, the one He called rock-like Peter, seemed to throw it all away. Judas had betrayed Jesus to the chief priests, but Peter had betrayed Him too, being too ashamed to admit being on His team.

JESUS IS ALIVE, AND SO ALL WHO TRUST IN HIM ARE BOUND TO HIM SO DEEPLY THAT WE THEREBY SHARE HIS LIFE. FOREVER.

Just as Jesus predicted. Can you imagine how Peter must have felt during these days after the resurrection? It was hanging over him, eating away.

## 3. Jesus reunited with an embarrassed deserter: Peter

So Jesus at last takes a quiet moment after the breakfast barbecue on the beach. The others are probably playing beach volleyball, and He takes Peter aside, and calls him by his original name, Simon, rather than his nickname of Peter. That in itself must have made Peter suspect something was up.

*'Simon son of John, do you truly love me more than these?'*

*'Yes, Lord … you know that I love you.' …*

*'Simon son of John, do you truly love me?'*

*… 'Yes, Lord, you know that I love you.'*

*'… do you love me?' …*

*'Lord, you know all things; you know that I love you.'*
*(21:15–17)*

Imagine the thousands of things going through Peter's head. 'What's He getting at? What does it mean? No wonder it says, in verse 17, he was hurt at the third time of asking. But that is John's way of drawing attention to the number, isn't it? Three questions = three chances. After three denials. I guess Peter was not just hurt, but acutely embarrassed. He knew. But more importantly, Jesus knew. And he knew that Jesus knew. And yet don't you think that at the same time, the wildest, strangest, most extraordinary, most radical thought began to creep into his mind. Not only did Jesus know about the betrayal - somehow, amazingly, it was ok.

> PETER KNEW. BUT MORE IMPORTANTLY, JESUS KNEW. AND HE KNEW THAT JESUS KNEW.

And then it would have dawned on him what Jesus said after each response. Feed my lambs; Take care of my sheep. Feed my sheep. You see, Peter, even Peter - the headstrong and overconfident deserter - still had a job to do. Even though it will have felt excruciating at the time, Peter will come to realise that Jesus was giving him the greatest and most loving gift he could have given him: a second chance. He'd messed up big time. But that was OK. Jesus knew all about it.

And even the prediction of the way he would die in v18-19 was an encouragement. Remember when at the Last Supper Jesus told them about his death. And Jesus replied:

Where I am going, you cannot follow now, but you will follow later (13:36)

Peter rashly responds:

Lord, Why can't I follow you now? I will lay down my life for you.

And Jesus asks him: Really? And at that point he predicts his 3 betrayals.

Do you see the echoes now? In v19 Jesus says: Follow me! And he knows he will. Peter will follow Jesus - to martyrdom. John has a slightly different future (as we see in the following verses); but that's not important now. Peter is restored and forgiven. And above all... trusted. Can you imagine the relief and joy?

We are so quick to write people off when they mess up. Especially when ministers mess up - and let's face it, we ministers mess up a lot. And too often, in the church, it is a question of one strike and you're out. Whereas that's not how Jesus treated Peter. And as we know from the rest of the New Testament, Peter would mess up on several occasions in the future.[9] The Lord Jesus is the God of the second chance and the 7th and the 707th. Now I know that trust is a very hard thing to regain when it is lost. And we

[9] e.g. Galatians 2:11-21

mustn't be naïve about this. But we mustn't be quick to reject those who fail so quickly. For Jesus isn't with us.

So as we close, what a privilege it is to have these three intensely personal conversations recorded. For they not only help us to believe that Jesus is the Christ – and thereby have life in his name. But they also show us the tender grace of the one who conquered death:

- A grieving friend is transformed – and given the task of being the first to tell the others
- An honest sceptic is transformed – and given the task of reaching those who have not seen
- An embarrassed deserter is transformed – and given the task of leading the believers.

But this is the mark of the Christ we've got to know. He is not only our Lord and God. He is also our loving friend.

## John 20-21 in overview

| Who? | Seeing & believing | Jesus' Identity | Background | A Job To Do? |
|---|---|---|---|---|
| **Why did John write? ...that you may believe that Jesus is the Christ, the son of God... have life in His name** | | | | |
| **JESUS reunited with a GRIEVING FRIEND: MARY MAGDALENE** | | | | |
| 20:1-9 **Mary Magdalene** | 20:1 Mary saw stone removed | 'Lord' probably only in sense of 'master' | | |
| **Simon Peter & Beloved Disciple** | 20:5 John looked at strips lying 20:6 Peter saw strips 20:8 John saw and believed - but neither got it from OT | | | |
| 20:10-18 **Mary Magdalene** | 20:11 Mary looked at tomb 20:14 Mary turned and saw Jesus - but didn't 'see' | They've taken the 'Lord' Rabboni 'Lord' now with fuller significance? | Cf. Luke 8.23 John 19:25 | 20:17 Go to the Brothers... tell them I am returning to my father and your Father; to my God and your God |
| **JESUS reunited with an HONEST SCEPTIC: THOMAS** | | | | |
| 20:19-23 **Disciples in Upper Room** | 20:20 Showed hands and side - disciples overjoyed when saw | Shalom Sent from Fa. Sends HS | | |
| 20:24-29 **Thomas in Upper Room** | 20:25 Unless I see... I will not believe 20:27 Touch and see my hands - 'stop being unbeliever, be believer' 20:29 you've seen and believed. Blessed who've not seen but believed... | Seen Lord? My Lord & My God | 11:16 - let us die with him 14:5 - how do we know the way | 20:29 Blessed are those who have not seen and yet have believed |
| 20:30-31 Jesus did many other miraculous signs in the presence of His disciples, which are not recorded in this book. But these are written that you may believe that Jesus is the Christ the Son of God, and that by believing you may have life in His name. | | | | |
| 21:1-12 **Simon Peter, Thomas, Nathanael, sons of Zebedee +2** | ANOTHER MIRACULOUS SIGN! 21:4 disciples didn't realize it was Jesus 21:14 appeared after raised | It's the Lord! | | |
| **JESUS reunited with and EMBARRASSED DESERTER: PETER** | | | | |
| 21:15-19 **Simon Peter** | 3 x do you love me? | Lord, you know I love you Lord, you know all things | 1:42 – Simon you will be Peter 13:36-38 – you can't follow me now but you will betray me x3 | 21:12, 16, 17 Feed my sheep 21:19 Follow me 21:22 You must follow me |
| 21:20-24 **Simon Peter & Beloved Disciple** | John will live long - and writes this testimony | | | |
| 21:25 Jesus did many other things as well. If every one of them were written down, I suppose that even the whole world would not have room for the books that would be written. | | | | |

# Further Reading

## Can You Believe The Resurrection?

Bruce, F F, *The New Testament Documents: Are They Reliable?*, IVP (2000 rev)

Morrison, Frank, *Who Moved The Stone?*, Authentic (2006)

Wenham, John, *Easter Enigma*, Paternoster (1984, 1996 rev)

Wright, N T, *Who Was Jesus?*, SPCK (2005 new ed)

## What Does The Resurrection Mean?

Allberry, Sam, *Lifted*, IVP (2010)

Carson, D A, *Scandalous*, IVP (2010)